NOW LOOK WHAT YOU'VE DONE!

NOW LOOK
WHAT YOU'VE DONE!

by Lee Lorenz

PANTHEON BOOKS

New York

All rights reserved under International and Pan-American Copy-
right Conventions. Published in the United States by Pantheon
Books, a division of Random House, Inc., New York, and simulta-
neously in Canada by Random House of Canada Limited, Toronto.

Library of Congress Cataloging in Publication Data

Lorenz, Lee, 1932– .
   Now Look What You've Done!

   1. American wit and humor, pictorial.
I. Title.
NC1429.L57A53   741.5'973   77-1145
ISBN 0-394-41552-3

Designed by Irva Mandelbaum

Manufactured in the United States of America

First Edition

For James Geraghty

NOW LOOK WHAT YOU'VE DONE!

"Nothing but smut today, Mrs. Trumbull."

"Mea Culpa, I'd like you to meet J'Accuse."

"The thing to bear in mind, gentlemen, is not just that Daisy has mastered a rudimentary sign language but that she can link these signs together to express meaningful abstract concepts."

*"Oh, you press the button down.
The data goes 'round and around,
Whoa-ho-ho-ho-ho-ho,
And it comes out here."*

"I'm sorry, Mr. Brodner, but I'm afraid there's no way we can
legally change you from a Libra to a Sagittarius."

"His Excellency the Lord High Muckity-Muck."

"At least you have something to look back on. Mine were all sins of <u>omission</u>."

"I left for work this morning and took a cab. When I got out, the driver said, 'Looks like a super day.' I walked into my office and my secretary offered me a Danish. 'Try one,' she said. 'They're super!' We had a staff meeting on the Brinton matter, which the chairman of the board characterized as 'super.' Roy Damon took me to lunch at what he called a 'super' little French place. I rode home with Bill Johnson and Ron McGruddy, who kept talking about some 'super' new film. As I came in, the doorman complimented me on my 'super' tie, and the elevator operator asked me if I didn't think we were having 'super' weather. My wife greeted me as I entered the apartment and said she had prepared a 'super' treat for dinner. I don't remember anything after that."

"When the sun goes down and the moon comes out,
The people gather round and they all begin to shout,
'Hey, hey, Uncle Dud, it's a treat to beat your feet on the Mississippi mud,
It's a treat to beat your feet on the Mississippi mud.'"

"When I said you should be easier on yourself, I didn't mean you should let yourself off scot-free."

*"That concludes my proposed remarks.
I will now fend off questions from
the audience."*

"At least be honest with yourself, Jamie. You're <u>never</u> going to be in the right mood to see 'Scenes from a Marriage.'"

"On the other hand, the Maitlands went by tramp steamer and loved every minute of it."

"Pardon my staring, but I'm trying to
get an intellectual fix on you."

"All I can say, Mr. Townsend, is thank goodness someone finally
had guts enough to bring lycanthropy out of the closet."

"Warrington Trently, this court has found you guilty of price-fixing, bribing a government official, and conspiring to act in restraint of trade. I sentence you to six months in jail, suspended. You will now step forward for the ceremonial tapping of the wrist."

HEADLINE-MAKERS
WARREN T. OAKLEY
BRIDGE CITY, IDAHO

Visiting the Soviet Union as a member of a U.S. trade mission, Mr. Warren T. Oakley was the central figure this week in a bizarre incident that threatened to have international repercussions. While strolling with his wife down Moscow's Tchaikovsky Street near the American Embassy, Mr. Oakley's hearing aid suddenly melted, singeing his left earlobe and ruining a recently purchased Siberian-sealskin topcoat. Although Soviet spokesmen officially denied that microwaves beamed at the Embassy to disrupt electronic-surveillance equipment were responsible, Mr. Oakley's hearing aid and coat were replaced by the Russian government, "in the spirit of détente." Neither Mr. Oakley nor his wife was available to the press, but a senior officer at the American Embassy said the matter was now officially closed.

HEADLINE-MAKERS
CHANG TSU-TSENG

The current upheaval in the People's Republic of China has demonstrated once again the pivotal role played in the Chinese political process by the slogans and songs that mysteriously flood the country at such times. Long thought to be the product of a special unit of the Central Committee, they are now known to be the work of one man, an obscure bureaucrat from Shansi Province named Chang Tsu-tseng. Working with only a brush, a sheaf of foolscap, and a slide whistle, Comrade Chang has for thirty years been both the Richard Rodgers and the Lorenz Hart of the People's Ongoing Struggle. During that period, he has produced literally hundreds of slogans, posters, chants, and songs, of which "Persevere, Comrades, and be brave! The teeth of the running dogs of revisionism cannot rend the pantaloons of a proletariat guided by the wisdom of Chairman Mao" is merely the best known. Comrade Chang lives quietly with his wife and three children in a government compound near Peking, where, during periods of political calm, he enjoys operating the switchboard. Although he has no ambition beyond "the inevitable triumph of Communism," Comrade Chang did express regret that "current circumstances" made it impossible for him to visit New York and shake hands with the "Daily News" man who wrote "Ford to City: Drop Dead."

"Good morning, Mr. Average Citizen. How would you like your goose cooked today?"

The Temptation of Saint Anthony

"Don't you love today's look? Everything goes with everything."

"Please don't thank me. I would have accepted a kickback from anyone."

"By George, the big bands are coming back!"

"We're all out of garni."

"Hey, Jack! is this the 'RR' train for Pelham Parkway?"

"There's no business like show business…"

"Harrison, whip me up a few off-the-cuff remarks on topics of general interest. My wife and I are socializing tonight."

"On the basis of these figures, Carter, your suggestion seems quite sound.

Certainly our expansion program is flexible enough to include these items.

However, on balance I think the proposal is premature.

Now, as to these figures on capital replacement…"

"Twenty-five nuclear submarines, twelve hundred ICBMs, two hundred and seventy-five cruise missiles—oops, wrong list."

"Howard, have you seen Ed? His
Adidas just came back without him."

"And so I say unto you, I'm
O.K., you're O.K.!"

"Amen, brother! You're O.K.
and we're O.K.!"

"It's not supposed to be any kind of look. It's just me."

*"Senior Vice-President Buffington reporting, sir. Requests permission
to advance and be recognized."*

"Here you are, Jack. Your signature on this simple document brings you your heart's desire. Check it out."

"Is that right? Around Remson Tool & Die, I daresay
I'm a bit of a cult figure myself."

"It's a great rhythm section, but the piano player's nowhere."

"'Genius' is an overused word, Berringer, but in this case nothing else fits."

"For the last time, no, I <u>don't</u> want to hear your private mantra."

"Mr. Feigle said, 'The hell with them. Let them take their damned dog food to another agency.' Mr. Bonister said, 'Done and done. By the way, Art, what have you done to your hair—it looks great!' Mr. Feigle said, 'It's this great new creme rinse—gives it lots of body.' Mr. Tolin said, 'I've used the same stuff and it didn't do diddley for me.' Mr. Remson said, 'You've got to work it in well.' Mr. Rogers said, 'Plain old soap and water's good enough for me.'…"

"Fantastic, isn't it? You just put on the jeans, sit in a
warm tub, and then let them dry to fit."

"I suppose the truth is <u>wherever</u> we live it's going to be a pestilential hole!"

"And a cultural note. The entire literary world turned out today to pay tribute to the novel, which died last night after a protracted illness."

"Oh, for Pete's sake, lady! Go ahead and touch it."

"We had planned to stay through August, but
their damn currency firmed up on us."

"I quack, therefore I am."

"Hate to bother you, but we wondered if you still had the other cushion."

"Well, I can see there __are__ differences to work out,
but basically I feel you have a sound
dog-and-little-old-lady relationship."

"Float like a butterfly, sting like a bee.
That's our prexy, old R. D."

"'More mulch'. That's your answer to everything!"

"Now, *about this twenty-four million, Henderson. Is that hush money,
slush money, or just something salted away for a rainy day?"*

"And so, extrapolating from the best figures available, we see that current trends, unless dramatically reversed, will inevitably lead to a situation in which the sky will fall."

"And now, having satisfied one hundred per cent of my daily requirements, I am returning to bed."

"Hi there, this is Libby. I'm out for the evening. Would you believe—two tickets for 'Private Lives.' But, thanks to the miracle of modern technology, you can leave a message. When you hear the little beep, start talking. You have thirty seconds to make your point. Hardly enough to get started, really. I know that if I were faced with that kind of deadline, I'd freeze up. Mike fright, I guess you'd call it. Anyway, if you can't think of anything cute to say, just leave your name and say when you'll call back. I'll be around tomorrow. No, wait a minute. In the morning, I'm off to Mr. John. Damn! Well, try in the afternoon then. I'll probably grab a bite downtown, which means I'll be back by three. Let's say three-thirty, to be on the safe side."

*"Please bear with me tonight, Licia. The old persona's
on the fritz, and I'm just lip-synching."*

"Beg pardon, sir, but I couldn't help noticing you were spiritually bereft."

"I've done some soft-core, some as-told-to's, and a few gothics. Right now I'm into psychohistory."

"After sports and the weather, we'll be back again with all the news all the time, day after day, year after year, forever and ever."

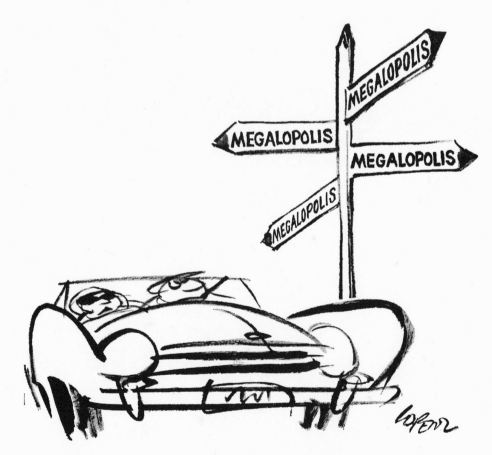

"Oh, for heaven's sake, Edgar! These days, everyone is foulmouthed."

"Confound it, Hawkins, when I said I meant that literally, that was just a figure of speech."

"How do I feel about being mugged? Well, naturally I didn't enjoy it and I certainly don't condone violence or threats of violence as a means toward social change. However, I can empathize with my assailant and realize that in his terms this is a valid response to the deteriorating socio-economic situation in which we find ourselves."

"Sweetheart, this is Rhona Dilmar. Rhona is one of our leading raunchy feminist poets."

"I'll bet you wouldn't have let me off so easily if I weren't a woman."

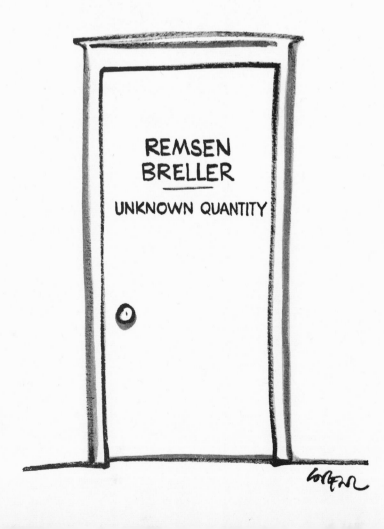

"They either have more taste than money or more money than
taste, but I can never remember which."

"I'm afraid, Son, this will never be yours. I'm having myself cloned."

"*I hope you don't mind. He doesn't know he's a dog.*"

"The blahs are here."

"The jury will disregard the witness's last remark."

"Hallelujah! I'm a bum!"

"I'll level with you, Fred. I was nobody till somebody loved me."

"Personally, I'm sick of running up brownie points. How
can I get my hands on some real cash?"

"You don't think it's <u>too</u> motley?"

"The wages are excellent, the fringe benefits are generous, and the people are extremely pleasant. No, I don't find it at all Kafkaesque."

"I just want you to know, R.B., how much I admire the way you out-
maneuvered Allied on that takeover without losing your femininity."

"It's hard to believe that just a few years ago they faced virtual extinction."

"That's funny. For some reason, I always thought of him as a liberal."

"Mr. Prentice is <u>not</u> your father. Alex Binster is <u>not</u> your brother. The anxiety you feel is <u>not</u> genuine. Dr. Froelich will return from vacation September 15th. Hang on."

"Now look what you've done!"

"Who the hell is Dizzy Gillespie, anyway?"

"I'll tell you what's missing from your game, Crowley—hate."

"Have you gentlemen concluded the decision-making process?"

"It's perfectly simple. <u>You</u> want to be loved. <u>I</u> want to be loved. Mobil Oil wants to be loved."

"My philosophy, gentlemen, is 'If it feels good, do it.' This feels good, by God, and I say do it."

"Buzz off, Louise! That was only till death us did part."

"That's funny. I'm sure it wasn't there when I dusted yesterday."

"My fun fur is no more fun."

"Isn't it fantastic? They take these plugs from the back of your neck and put them on top of your head, and six months later it's a whole new ballgame."

"I'm sorry, my son, but I'm afraid we Wasps have
no tribal wisdom to pass on."

*"I was bringing you one perfect rose, but the
engine conked out in Darien."*

"Be patient. When your time comes, we'll call you."

"I understand you are a gifted child. I was a gifted child myself."

"*Grayson is a liberal in social matters, a conservative in economic matters, and a homicidal psychopath in political matters.*"

"What with the population crunch and all, we're just reproducing
ourselves and letting it go at that."

*"By George, Harkins, you've got integrity! And I don't
mean post-Watergate integrity, either."*

ABOUT THE AUTHOR

Lee Lorenz has been drawing cartoons ever since he was a youngster, and over the years his work has appeared in practically every American magazine to publish that genre. Since 1973 he has been the *New Yorker*'s art editor and the cartoons in this book, all of which were originally published in the *New Yorker*, constitute the first collection of his work since HERE IT COMES, published nearly ten years ago.